●

SETH MASIA
Technical Editor, *SKI Magazine*

●

Photographs by
TOM LIPPERT

●

Demonstrations by
Chris Fellows
Supervisor, Squaw Valley Ski School

A Fireside Book
Published by Simon & Schuster
New York   London   Toronto   Sydney   Tokyo   Singapore

SKi

MAGAZINE'S

MANAGING

THE MOUNTAIN

TOP TIPS FOR MASTERING CHALLENGING TERRAIN

FIRESIDE
Simon & Schuster Building
Rockefeller Center
1230 Avenue of the Americas
New York, New York, 10020

FIRESIDE and colophon are registered trademarks
of Simon & Schuster Inc.

Designed by Chris Welch
Manufactured in the United States of America

10 9 8 7 6 5 4 3 2 1

Library of Congress Cataloging in Publication Data

Masia, Seth.
    Ski magazine's Managing the mountain: top tips for mastering the
    challenging terrain / Seth Mesia : photographs by Tom Lippert; dem-
    onstrations by Chris Fellows.
        p.   cm.
    "A Fireside book."
    Includes index.
    1. Skis and skiing. I. Lippert, Tom. II. Ski (New York, N.Y.)
    III. Title. IV. Title: Managing the mountain.
    GV854.M315   1992
    796.93—dc20   92-17034
                                                                  CIP

ISBN: 0-671-75082-8

CONTENTS

ACKNOWLEDGMENTS

This book owes its existence to the skiers who taught me to teach: Pete Gorrel, Dick Dorworth, Leroy Hill, Lito Tejada-Flores, Jorg Dutschke, Tom Lippert, Tony Hardy, John Kirschner, Jim Kercher, Kathleen Hesler, Stu Campbell, Mike Porter, Tim Petrick and Mike Sodergren.

I'm grateful to the gang at SKI Magazine, whose toil and woe amid the flatlanders of New York give me the freedom to live and teach in the mountains. Special thanks to Dick Needham, Steve Cohen, George Bauer and Ed Pitoniak, for their encouragement over the years.

Thanks to Kara Leverte and Angela Miller, who planted the seed for this book in my head.

I had the misfortune to break a leg in a ski race just as we began planning the book. Tom Lippert and Chris Fellows worked hard to produce the photographs, matching the text precisely. They know enough about my work habits to have gone off and done most of the job without me.

My wife Stacey tolerated with unflagging good humor the

weeks when I shut my office door against the cheerful family chaos outside. Stacey is a very good skier, but the couloirs of Val Morel and Les Arcs scared her. In a sense I wrote the book for her.

FOREWORD

How's your snow vocabulary? Mine includes sleet, junk, powder, breakable crust, windblown, crud, corn, hail, sierra cement, ice. The Eskimos, it is said, have separate words for over thirty-five different types of snow, which tells me that natural snow comes in at least that many flavors. And Eskimos don't have machines or skier traffic to create packed powder, corduroy, man-made, moguls, cut-up or slush bumps. If you figure in these "artificial" conditions, you can probably add another two-dozen words for snow. Which means that each time you go skiing, you might encounter any of sixty different snow types. If you're a weekend skier who rides the lifts ten to fifteen days a year, chances are you'll never ski the same conditions twice in a season.

Think about the snow you've skied in. There's light new snow fallen on hard ice, requiring a different ski technique than light new snow lying on packed powder. There's new heavy snow on top of a light crust layer. There's old snow warmed by the sun. There's old light snow that's been packed by 50 mph wind. Each type of snow has its own feel under your skis; each requires a subtly different touch.

Unfortunately, modern skiing has spoiled many skiers. Grooming machines rob these different types of snow by churning them into a homogeneous, smooth, predictable, easy-to-ski carpet. Which is great—some of the time. Groomed runs are especially good for the beginning of the year, or for the first turns of the day when you're getting your timing back and your feet under you. But the ease and comfort of these tilted billiard tables keeps many skiers from enjoying the whole mountain.

It's the unique personality of each day's snow, along with the challenge of varied terrain, that makes skiing a sensuous thrill. It's great snow on a spectacular mountainside that produces an epic day.

Now, I've had some great days skiing on groomed terrain. But never my best days. And a smoothly groomed slope hardly ever inspires the kinds of hoots and hollers you hear as powder skiers blast down a steep bowl. No, all my really memorable days have come when the snow and mountain combine into something unique: two feet of light new snow in an open bowl, or an inch of corn on a smooth face, or big soft powder bumps, or heavy cut-up crud in a steep couloir, or a rolling glade in the midst of a blizzard. Those are the days I remember.

Happily, you can ski all these conditions and varied terrain using basically the same turn. A few small variations and tricks adapt the parallel turn for easy skiing in challenging situations. And that's what this book is about.

If you're an advanced skier when the slope is manicured, but you regress to the intermediate or even beginner level when the conditions are adverse or the terrain is scary, then this book could open the door to a much broader, more exhilarating ski experience.

Not only will skiing become more fun and exciting as you gain confidence off the groomed runs, but a whole new world of skiable terrain will open up. This is especially true on big mountains and in Europe, where only a small percentage of the terrain is ever groomed.

Groomed runs are undeniably fun, but even here the snow doesn't stay carpet-smooth all day. The groomed runs are at their best early in the morning, when the surface is still silky corduroy. As the day goes on, this surface deteriorates under skier traffic, and gradually develops bumps and slick spots. The skier who doesn't enjoy imperfect snow may never ski right up until the lifts close.

I like skiing in all conditions; obviously, some are more fun than others. The biggest benefit to learning how to ski all kinds of snow is that you can choose the best available snow on any particular day. For example, if it's foggy and impossible to see on the open slopes, you can move into the trees. When the snow is so thick and heavy that turning is a chore on moderate slopes, you move to the steeper slopes and let gravity do the hard work. When the bumps are rock hard and choppy, and there's frozen crud in the bowls, then you arc turns on the groomed runs. There is always something good to ski, somewhere on the mountain. And if you're versatile enough to ski it all, you'll never have a bad day. Cascade concrete, powder bumps, wind slab, bottomless powder. It's time to expand your vocabulary.

—Mike Hattrup
1992

1
HOW TO USE
THIS BOOK

I call it mogul shock, and it has overtaken every skier at one time or another. You stand at the top of some horrific run as your friends disappear far below, and a sense of panic creeps into your soul. You might ask, "How am I going to get down this with dignity?" In an extreme case, you might ask, "How am I going to get down this in one piece?"

Mogul shock doesn't happen only at the top of mogul runs. It also happens at the top of steep bowls, at the top of broad fields of glistening perfect powder, at the top of narrow funnels, at the top of the race course, at the top of a sheet of glare ice—at the top of any run that makes you nervous. If you haven't skied a lot of bumps, or steeps, or bottomless powder, or couloirs, or slalom courses, or ice, then any of those things might make you pause and wonder what to do next.

SKI Magazine's *Managing the Mountain* is meant to be a helpful companion as you ski unfamiliar ground. When you run into a challenge on the hill—some combination of difficult slope and snow conditions you haven't mastered—this book should provide some helpful hints on getting down safely, and maybe even with style.

The book is not meant to substitute for a ski instructor. The lessons and ideas outlined here have been borrowed from some of the top ski teaching pros in the U.S. I use these lessons frequently when I teach at Squaw Valley. But lessons work best when you have a competent instructor to demonstrate how a maneuver works and then coach you through it. So your best tactic when in over your head on difficult terrain is to find a certified member of Professional Ski Instructors of America (PSIA) and ask for a critique and lesson.

But there are times when you ski on your own, without an instructor or friendly expert to offer advice about difficult terrain. For these moments, it's nice to have some help right there in your pocket. And that's when you'll reach for this book.

Each chapter in this book deals with a specific terrain or snow problem. And each chapter is divided into advice for relatively new skiers (the circle), for intermediate skiers (the square) and for advanced skiers (the diamond). Even expert skiers understand that in unfamiliar conditions they may have to back off a notch—a hot shot Vermonter who has spent years mastering icy bumps may feel like a low intermediate during a first encounter with airy, bottomless Utah powder, and the Colorado cruiser may go to pieces when asked to blast through a rock-hard New England slalom course. So use the advice that seems appropriate and accessible, regardless of the skill grade attached.

If you're a beginner: If you have friends who ski, you already know that the sport is addictive. They prove it every weekend, by driving for hours through lousy weather to get that skiing fix. And they probably want you to join in, which proves the disease communicable.

See a few ski films and you'll understand the overwhelming sensations—of speed, freedom, weightlessness—that hook people on skiing. I'll let your ski-addicted friends talk you into trying the sport for the first time. But I'd like to pass along some advice on learning to ski quickly and painlessly.

Certain flatland sports are wonderful preparation for skiing. In general, athletes who are used to balancing on a slippery surface learn to ski easily. These include skaters and hockey players, surfers, skateboarders, boardsailers, waterskiers and roller skaters and rollerbladers. If you perform any of those sports with finesse, you belong on skis. If you're accustomed to sports that depend on good traction (tennis, basketball and so on), you may still belong on skis, but be prepared for some new sensations. You'll spend your first day on the slopes just learning to keep your skis underneath you.

In fact, if you have never skied before, it will help to spend a few hours ice skating or cross-country skiing before you take your first lesson on downhill skis. That will teach you to balance easily on flat terrain before you face the problem of balancing on a hillside.

Take lessons at a recognized ski school—look for the striped-shield logo of the Professional Ski Instructors of America (or the Canadian Ski Instructors Alliance). Don't let a friend, lover or spouse teach you to ski, unless you are ready for a major screaming match in public. Egos get rubbed raw when an inexperienced instructor shouts confusing advice to a rattled beginner. Remember when your father tried to teach you to drive stick-shift? Learning to ski is potentially much worse. You're far better off with a good-humored, tolerant professional instructor.

Most ski schools begin lessons at 10:00 or 11:00 A.M. This gives students an hour or two in the morning to get organized and warm up before joining class. In real life, two hours on a busy Saturday morning is barely enough time to park the car, buy tickets, rent equipment and find the ski school meeting place. This is because most ski resorts are set up not for the lost, confused beginner but for the convenience of experienced skiers who want to get to the fresh powder at the crack of dawn.

So rent your ski equipment on Friday, and beat the morning rush on Saturday. Friday night, walk around the house in your ski boots for an hour or so to get used to them. If possible, buy your lift and lesson tickets in advance. Often this can be accomplished by calling the ski school on Friday afternoon. On Saturday, get up early enough to find a parking space near the base lodge. Then you'll have time for an extra cup of coffee and some stretching exercises before lesson time.

Arrive for your first lesson properly equipped. Wear water repellent ski pants. You'll find yourself sitting down in the snow frequently, and the pants will keep you dry and warm instead of wet and cold. Wear good, warm leather gloves, a comfortable parka, and a knit wool hat. Be sure to bring a sturdy pair of sunglasses or ski goggles, and carry a tube of sunblock lotion.

New skiers usually rent skis, boots and poles for the first few days. Make sure the boots fit properly: They should be comfortable but very snug. Your toes should have room to wiggle, but the ball of the foot, the instep, arch, and heel should be immobile in the boot. Learn how to buckle the boots properly, and buckle them just tight enough to support the foot solidly. Overtightening the boots will cut off circulation to your toes, leading to cold feet, and will make the boots so stiff you'll lose the ability to flex your ankles forward. As you'll see, you'll need that ankle flex to control your skis and your speed. If you wear orthotic insoles in your running or tennis shoes, use them in your ski boots, too. Poles should reach just above your elbow (later, as you improve, you'll get shorter poles). Make sure the skis are in good shape. The plastic bottoms should be smooth and clean, the edges smooth and just sharp enough to shave a little dust off your fingernail. Most first-day skiers can use 160 centimeter skis (men) or 150 centimeter skis (women). Make sure the people in the rental shop show you how to step in and out of the bindings.

During your first hour on skis, you'll learn how to balance, walk and climb. During your first day, you'll learn to glide, slow down, stop and turn. You'll also learn to ride the lift. Inevitably, you'll learn how to fall safely, and how to get up from a fall.

By the end of your second day, you should feel comfortable making linked wedge turns on gentle, groomed terrain. You should be able to traverse (ski across the hill), glide in control down the fall line (straight down the hill), steer around obstacles (especially other skiers), and move your weight comfortably both forward and back and from ski to ski.

By the third day, most reasonably athletic people can begin making wedge turns at a brisker pace, on steeper terrain. Centrifugal force causes the tails of the skis to skid downhill near the end of the turn. At this point the skid tends to tighten the turn, helping to control your speed. A skidded turn is called a "christie," after Christiania, the old name for Oslo, Norway, where the turn was first demonstrated 120 years ago. Once you've learned to control this skid, you're ready for the green circle (beginner) exercises in this book.

If you're an experienced skier: At various stages of our skiing career, we all reach a learning plateau. Some folks are simply comfortable at a certain level and feel no particular ambition to move up to the next stage of expertise. Others (perhaps the more competitive among us) find stasis frustrating. They want to ski more difficult terrain without that queasy feeling of imminent disaster. They want mastery of the sport.

Reasons for plateauing are various. The most common is simply lack of time. If you have a full-time career in the city, it's tough to spend enough days on the hill to achieve true expertise. (Let's face it: most real experts got that way by skiing full time, even if that was during a misspent youth.)

Short of quitting your job and moving to Aspen, the cure for the lack-of-time plateau is to plan a couple of ski vacations around a structured program of instruction. Most major ski areas offer week-long advanced skier clinics and adult race camps. These concentrated courses work—just ask about the proportion of happy customers who come back every couple of years for a refresher.

Another cause for plateau stalling is physical. It's easy to see why a desk-bound skier might not be strong enough muscularly, to power the ski into expert-level maneuvers, or aerobically, for the lung capacity to ski hard for hours at high altitudes. Skiing is, after all, a sport, and it requires physical conditioning as other sports do. The only solution here is hard work, in the gym and on the road. Leg strength comes from an intelligent weight training program—make sure it includes exercises for rotational and edging power, as well as the usual quadricep and gluteal workouts. Aerobic capacity derives from the appropriate hours of running, cycling, rowing, stair climbing or dance. At the very least, find a way to walk for an uninterrupted forty minutes a day.

A common problem is psychological; many people are uncomfortable with the higher speeds associated with steep terrain. The average recreational skier potters along at about 12 mph, an astonishingly modest velocity for what we generally consider a "thrill" sport. The fact is that, even if you're comfortable at 65 mph on the interstate, speed is a much different thing when you've got your feet on the ground and no steel cage, seatbelt or airbag to protect your soft body. If you're not at ease with speed, try acclimating around home by bicycling or rollerblading. You'll generally move at about 15 mph on the flat (very strong athletes can average 20 to 25 mph) but gradually you'll become more comfortable with wind whistling past your ears.

A related syndrome is fear of heights. I'm astounded at the number of students who tense up on the ski lift or at the top of a steep pitch. In most folks, this mild fear of heights is connected to a fear of losing control, and it disappears when they discover that good ski technique enables them to descend steep terrain in full control—and without embarrassment. (However, people who are clinically phobic about heights probably shouldn't ski unless accompanied by a licensed therapist.)

Now here's a secret. By far the overriding reason people plateau is improper equipment. Some common examples:

▲ The intermediate simply can't learn to carve an expert-level turn on beginner equipment: the soft, floppy skis are designed to skid instead of arc, and the flexible boots are designed to forgive errors rather than to transmit aggressive edging forces.

▲ The light adult can't load the center of the ski adequately in boots that are too large or too stiff. Such boots lock the ankle, forcing the skier into an inelegant "toilet turn" on the ski tails.

▲ The young skier can't progress on skis that are too long or too stiff, because he can't decamber them into a clean round turn and must rely instead on "leapers" to unweight the ski between turns.

▲ A strong skier using soft-flexing boots can't get the full measure of performance from a race ski, because the boot allows too much forward motion at the end of the turn. This unloads the tail, producing a skidding "abstem" of the outside ski.

▲ If your poles are too long, the pole plant tends to rock you back onto your heels; if they're too short, you tend to lean far forward or hunker down for the pole plant. Strapless sabre-style grips often force a skier to cock the wrist and swing the whole arm for the pole plant, a gross motion that can upset the balance of a smooth, subtle turn.

If you've been working hard to get off a plateau, with little success, look carefully at your equipment. If you chose your boots for their soft and comfortable flex, now you might need a firmer high-performance model. If you've been reluctant to commit to a longer ski, maybe it's time to move up to a ski designed for the way you want to ski next year, instead of sticking with the ski you learned on. If your friends or instructors are always yelling at you to get off the tails of your skis, maybe you could use a boot soft enough to free your ankles. And if you just can't drive your ski edges into the ice, or the skis feel awkward and inconsistent, maybe it's time to have them stone ground and tuned.

Boot problems are best handled with the help of a professional fitter, at a ski shop that's willing to guarantee boot fit. In particular, look for a shop knowledgeable in making custom footbeds (sometimes called orthotics) and measuring cant requirements. Similarly, for help in selecting and tuning skis, rely on the shop with the best reputation for custom ski tuning.

It's simple enough to find out who does the best work in a ski town. Just ask the local "ski bums," meaning the folks who work on the mountain and in the restaurants. In a big city, it's trickier. Visit a few ski shops, and talk to the mechanics in the back room (if there is no back room, find out where the shop sends its work). Trust your skis and boots to a shop where the people who do the work are good, enthusiastic skiers themselves.

Assuming your gear is in good shape, that you're in good physical condition and psychologically attuned to moving up to the next degree of difficulty, the next step is to visualize what needs to happen as you overcome mogul shock. Coaches in every sport now understand the value of visualization, and a major goal in sports training today is to teach the athlete to anticipate making all the right moves. The body does tend to go where the mind's eye sends it. One of the purposes of this book is to help you visualize the next step in the vertical dance we call skiing.

2
THE TOOLS

TERRAIN, GRAVITY AND YOUR SKIS CAN DO ALL THE WORK

Experts make skiing look easy. That's because they've figured out how to avoid all the hard work.

Yes, skiing is a sport, and to learn it requires a certain level of physical conditioning, especially in leg strength and lung capacity. But have you ever noticed that really good skiers—people capable of fluid, effortless runs over the most difficult terrain—rarely get winded?

The fact is that people who ski efficiently don't have to work very hard. They've learned how to ski in control, moving with the mountain instead of against it. They don't use a lot of muscle power to push their skis around. Instead, they've found out that gravity and terrain can be used to start almost any turn, and that the shape and flex of the ski can be used to finish almost any turn. Let the mountain and the equipment do the work, and you won't have to. John Kirschner, one of the veteran instructors in the Vail Ski School, sums it up neatly: "Skiing is a gravity-feed sport," he says. "If you do it right, you don't sweat."

Most skiers, unfortunately, have occasion to sweat buck-
ets. Whenever you're nervous about the terrain or the snow,
you tend to crank your skis around hard, using all the muscle you can muster. You know instinctively that safety lies in
getting those skis through the turn and back across the hill,
into the traverse position where they can be used as brakes.
So you do everything you can to get the turn started quickly
and finished early. You jump high to clear the skis from the
snow, pivot madly in the air, and come down with the skis
pointed more or less across the fall line in the other direction. It's essentially a Michael Jordan leap, except that when
Jordan goes up he's carrying no more than three pounds of
basketball, shoe leather and uniform, while you, you poor
skier, are dragging 20 pounds of equipment and four layers
of heavy winter clothing. No wonder you sweat.

Watch the good skiers. They never jump, and yet they
manage to make crisp short turns. The secret is that they
have an advantage over Michael Jordan: they're not playing
on a flat court.

On gentle terrain, new skiers and intermediate skiers are
taught to rise up tall to start a new turn. Standing tall does
two things: It flattens the skis on the snow, disengaging the
edges so the skis can be steered toward the new turn. And it
momentarily lightens the skis (a phenomenon we call unweighting), which also serves to make steering easier. Of
course, rising tall means lifting the entire upper body a few
inches, using leg strength to do it. That's work, and if you do
it all day long you'll feel tired.

Expert skiers get tall to start their turns, but only on
perfectly smooth, basketball-court terrain. Where the trail
has rolls, banks, bumps, holes, shelves or ruts, experts use
the snow surface for unweighting. Ski over any convex roll
in the snow and, if you're moving fast enough, you'll feel
your skis get light on the backside of the bump. In effect, the
bump has unweighted your skis. At this moment, it's a sim

Up un-weighted parallel turn

ple matter to change edges. Voilà, you've started a new turn—without lifting your body or even straightening your legs. All you've done is shift your knees a few inches sideways. You've just bought a turn (or the beginning of one, anyway) for free. No sweat so far.

You can practice terrain unweighting on any gently rolling ski slope. Before starting out, look downhill. Pick a gentle bump a little to one side of the trail. Ski straight to that bump, and as you reach its top—as you feel your skis lighten on the other side—change edges and begin a turn. Look ahead and pick your next bump, over on the other side of the trail. Each gentle bump you encounter can be the beginning of a new turn.

Terrain unweighting

What happens on steep terrain where there are no bumps? Experts have an answer for that, too. The whole point of unweighting is to release pressure on the skis, and you do this by moving the body relative to the surface of the snow. If the surface is tilted sharply, you can unweight the skis by moving your upper boy outward or even downward. It takes nerve and commitment, but it's how expert skiers change edges on steep terrain—by reaching far downhill for the pole plant. Because the upper body moves with gravity instead of against it, this is an efficient, low-energy way to release the edges and begin a turn. Another term for this downhill projection of the upper body is crossover, because the body crosses over the skis.

Crossover turn initiation

With more practice, you can pick your turn-bumps or crossover points two or three turns in advance, and pick them along the route you want to ski. You'll soon find yourself following along with the shape of the trail, letting the mountain establish your rhythm. It's a delightful sensation, running in harmony with the hill instead of battling gravity. It's skiing like a flowing stream, gravity fed.

Okay, we've got the turn started. But what about speed control? If you simply flow like water, won't you accelerate like Niagara? Well, yes. And that's where finishing the turn comes in.

The end of the ski turn is where all the braking happens. After all, at the beginning of the turn all we do is steer the skis downhill, into the position where they want to accelerate. (This is why we're so anxious to get the start of the turn over with and the skis pointed back in a sane, across-the-hill, finishing position.) After the skis cross through the fall line (it takes just half a second), we want them to arc smoothly into a round, controlled, edged platform, gripping the snow in opposition to the momentum built up in our half-second of acceleration.

It certainly would help if the skis were designed to turn by themselves. And in fact, that's exactly how they are designed.

The ski's shape (its gentle hourglass figure) and flex pattern (the ski is a long, lively spring) combine to make a neat

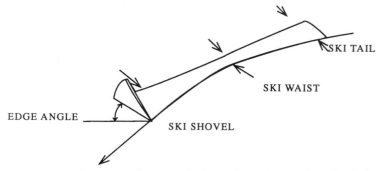

Ski sidecut—because of its gentle hourglass shape, the edged ski makes a smooth arc in the snow.

arc on the snow, but only when the ski is edged and pressured. Once you've changed edges on top of that long, gentle bump, you can simply hold the outside ski up on edge and balance against it. Then the ski will make a clean round turn for you, sweet as can be. It's just like leaning a bicycle into a turn.

Notice that I said "outside" ski. The parallel skier has edged both skis, but as the edges begin to bite into the snow your momentum (your angular momentum, to be precise) compresses the center of the ski with a force you feel through the legs. We commonly describe this sensation as centrifugal force. Centrifugal force pushes the body "outward," away from the center of the turn. It's the same force you bank against when you corner that bicycle, the force that makes the car sway onto its left tires when you corner hard to the right.

Resist centrifugal force by standing on the outside ski and rolling it onto a higher edge. Standing on just one ski (actually, just on the thin, steel edge of one ski) requires a fine

Centrifugal force

sense of balance, but it also concentrates your weight on a single sharp edge for better grip on hard snow, and bends the single ski into a deeper arc for a shorter turn.

The shorter the turn, the more centrifugal force you'll have to resist. That means you'll use more leg strength. But even so, with your skis slicing cleanly through the snow instead of skidding sideways, you'll do less total work. You won't have to correct constantly using the entire body to keep your balance, because with this smooth, carved turn there's little chance you'll lose your balance in the first place. After all, you're simply following the ski along its length, by far its most stable dimension. If skis were really meant to go sideways, they'd be turned up at the edges instead of in front.

If the ski slices forward instead of skidding sideways, you might well ask where the braking action comes from. It comes from completing the turn; from bringing your arc across the hill and away from the accelerating fall line. Point your skis straight downhill, you go faster. Point them across the hill, you slow down. Point them back up the hill, you stop. Simple. Speed control in the carved turn is a matter of rounding out the turn until you reach a comfortable speed and then, as you reach the next roll, starting another turn.

So let the terrain and gravity do your unweighting. Let the ski edge round out the turn for speed control. Don't work at all.

The trick is in learning the sense of timing, the fine balance skills and the ability to read terrain. Acquiring this skillfulness requires lots of miles and some hard work. Chapter three contains some exercises to help develop the physical know-how you'll need to ski with gravity feed.

When it all comes together, the effortless rhythm of it turns out to be the most addictive element of skiing. Rhythm proves to be a vital element in learning to ski. Establish a rhythm, and the muscles gradually learn to do their own thinking, as they do when you dance. That leaves your brain

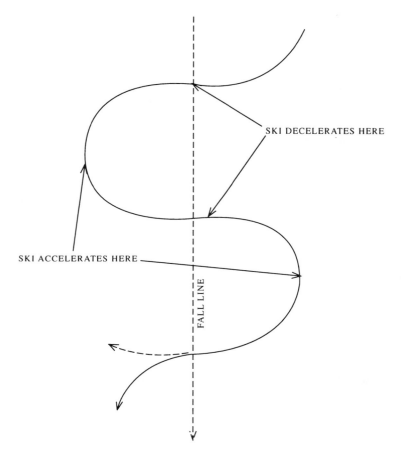

Control speed by completing the turn.

free to pick your route and watch for obstacles. Meanwhile, your legs are learning a progressively simpler set of commands: Cross the roll, get light, change edges, steer, compress, ride around on the ski. Roll, light, steer, compress. Light, steer, compress. Light, compress. Light, compress. Light, compress. All the way down the run.

That's the theory. Let's go skiing.

3
BASIC FORM

HOW TO
ACHIEVE
BALANCE AND
EFFICIENCY

You can't get the mountain and your skis to do the work for you until you've achieved a comfortable, consistently balanced position. Until you can maintain that position easily, you'll burn far too much energy recovering from every little upset and skid. Once you've found a centered, stable stance, though, the skis will work naturally and easily. In fact, whenever we talk about modifying a body position, the goal will be to bring the skis into a more efficient placement on the snow.

GREEN

AN ATHLETIC STANCE

What sports are you good at? Do you play tennis? Basketball? Touch football? Do you swim? In almost every sport,

there's a "ready" position. Think about a tennis player standing at the baseline, waiting for the serve to come zinging over
the net. The player stands on the balls of his feet, feet placed
about shoulder-width apart. Ankles, knees and hips are
flexed slightly. Eyes are fixed straight ahead, on the ball.
Hands, too, are in front, gripping the racket.

*"Ready" position—the basic stance on skis with all joints flexed
slightly and hands forward*

In this position, the tennis player is ready to move quickly in any direction; forward to the net, back to the fence, right or left to use a forehand or backhand swing. He can pivot or leap; joints and muscles are coiled, ready to spring. In football, the linebacker waiting for the snap stands in the same position. So does the basketball player guarding an opponent, or the wrestler getting set to grapple. Even a swimmer, ready to dive off the edge of the pool, begins much this way.

The ready position is the start of a good position on skis. We'll modify it slightly to allow for the fact that the playing floor isn't level. But to start, find a flat spot in the snow and drop into a loose, relaxed ready position: Skis are about hip-width apart and parallel. Balance is on the arches of both feet, the skis weighted equally. Ankles are slightly flexed (shins rest very lightly against the boot tongue). Knees and hips are flexed, back erect but not stiff. Eyes look ahead, watching where you propose to go. Hands are forward, just in front of the toe bindings, at roughly waist level (you should be able to see your hands without directly looking downward).

Stay loose, ready to absorb terrain variations as your skis glide forward. From this position try stepping sideways and forward. Lean forward, pushing hard against the boot tongues to make your boots flex. Now lean back, pressuring the tails of the skis. Return to a centered, ready stance, and roll your knees from side to side, feeling how your edges work on the snow. Rise tall and sink low by flexing both your ankles and knees together; as you sink, the boots should flex a little, so that you drop straight toward the middle of the ski. As you rise tall, weight can move a little forward onto the ball of the foot, (this will help you steer the skis into a new turn), but as you sink low the weight should come back onto the arch of the foot.

Now let's move this position onto a gently pitched run. Put your skis across the fall line, into the traverse position.

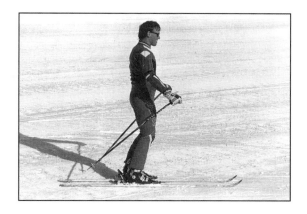

Flex ankles and knees together when you sink low.

Resume the ready stance. This time one foot is a bit lower than the other, due to the slope. Assume it's the right foot on the downhill side. Because of the way your knees bend, the left foot will scoot a few inches forward. The left knee goes forward, and so does the left hip, the left shoulder, and the left hand. You're in a ready stance, but your belly, chest and eyes are all pointed a bit downhill. Because your upper body projects downhill, a little more weight falls on the right ski.

Remember to stay loose. Glide across the hill in this position and try lifting the uphill ski right off the snow, just for a moment. If your position is stable, balancing on the down-hill ski should be no problem. If, when you lift the uphill ski, you tend to fall uphill, turn the shoulders and hips and hands to face farther downhill, and try again.

As you glide across the hill, experiment with rolling on and off the edge of the downhill ski. Do this by moving the downhill knee sideways: turn the knee uphill to get a higher edge angle, and downhill to flatten the ski.

As you roll the knee uphill, you should find that the ski

Roll the knees uphill to put the skis on edge; roll them downhill to flatten the ski and begin a new turn.

begins to turn uphill and slow down. As you roll the knee downhill, the ski will flatten and begin to skid. If you steer the ski at the same time, the ski will begin to point downhill and you'll accelerate into a turn.

Try this traversing exercise several times in each direction, lifting the uphill ski and rolling the downhill knee. As you get comfortable with the idea of controlling the direction of the traverse by controlling the edge angle of the ski, you can begin to link some long, rhythmic turns together using edge angle alone.

Don't force the turn. If you roll both knees into the new turn together, as the skis go through the fall line you'll speed up. Keep the shoulders, hips and hands pointed downhill, and your weight will naturally shift onto the new outside ski. Wait for the ski to complete the turn for you—don't push it. On gentle terrain you can get away with this "patience" turn: just hold the turn until it comes around into the new traverse position and begins to slow down.

Always finish the turn in your comfortable, ready stance. From there it's easy to get tall, flatten the skis, and steer into a new turn. Once the turn is started, just flex the ankles and knees slowly to resume the ready stance.

When you can do a dozen of these turns comfortably and with consistent rhythm, move onto slightly steeper terrain and try it again. Where the slope is steeper the beginning of the turn happens more quickly, because the snow creates less resistance to gravity. But the end of the turn happens more quickly, too, because it's easier to get the skis up on a higher edge angle. So your turns become shorter and quicker, just what you want on steeper terrain, where braking becomes more important.

Patience turn

B L U E

TURN SHAPE FOR SPEED CONTROL

You already know how to make a round, smooth and stable turn on relatively easy terrain. The problem is that when the trail turns steep, many skiers resort to old habits. They push the outside ski away on a stiff leg and get a ragged, braking skid, or they over-rotate so the body leans uphill.

To keep that comfortable round arc, remember that there are basically two ways to slow down: skidding; or carving the turn all the way around until the ski points across (or even up) the hill. On steeper terrain, where the turn starts more easily, you have the opportunity of beginning the turn finish earlier. And that means you can get the ski across the hill sooner and begin slowing sooner. We're still talking about a round turn, but with a tighter, smaller arc.

An easy way to tighten the turn is to let the ski tails skid smoothly. A simple way to do this is to unload the tails, together. Instead of pushing on the heels to break the bond between edge and snow, press forward just a bit onto the balls of your feet. This motion drives the edges deeper into the snow at the ski tip, but releases pressure on the ski tails, allowing them to slide sideways. As the tails swing out, you get a braking effect. In addition, the turn shortens and you'll quickly find the skis in a traverse.

To stop the skid, do these things simultaneously, gently and smoothly: stand on the outside (downhill) ski, center your weight on the arch of that foot, and roll the knees (especially the outside knee) toward the center of the turn. Unless the snow is bulletproof ice, the ski edge will bite and round out the turn nicely.

To get the fine edge control you need to go from a steered

turn entry to a tail skid to a carved-turn exit, you'll need to finish the turn in a good, flexed, ready stance: eyes and hands pointed downhill, ankles and knees flexed. You simply cannot edge a ski if the knees are too straight—the legs don't bend that way.

Experiment with skidded parallel turns, starting with a pure carved patience turn (a turn with no sideways braking component) and working down in progressively shorter turns with more and more skid. The skid starts when the skis pass the fall line (that is, when they're pointing straight downhill); the two skis should skid smoothly and at the same time.

Look back up at your tracks. If you felt smoothly balanced in the turn, your tracks in the snow will show a smooth round arc. If you felt ragged, your tracks will look uneven.

All the motions to establish and end the skid are subtle. All it takes is a degree or two of roll with the knee and an almost invisible rocking of the weight from arch to ball of foot. In fact from here on, many of the edge control and pressure control exercises we do will take place inside the ski boot, where no one can even see them. Actually, this is one of the things that makes expert skiers seem so smooth. The corrections they do make are subtle, and hidden in the boot.

Practice the round, skidded turn until you can make short, medium and long turns, smoothly and rhythmically, on steep, groomed terrain.

Skidded parallel turn

B L A C K

Pressure Control

The advanced skier won't use the skidded portion of the round, shaped turn. Instead, the expert keeps the tail of the ski engaged for solid edgehold at the end of the turn.

To start the turn, the expert releases pressure on the edged downhill ski, changing edges at the same moment. This is easy to do with a smooth crossover motion, helped along with the pole plant. The crossover (moving the upper body across the skis toward the bottom of the hill) goes with the pole plant. It's simply natural to use the reach-forward motion of the pole plant to trigger motion of the upper body in the same direction.

As you reach forward and downhill, the knees and feet rotate downhill, too, releasing the edges and steering the skis toward the fall line. And because your upper body is leading the parade, as the skis turn downhill your weight moves onto the *ball* of the foot.

As the skis point down the fall line, let them accelerate back under your center so your weight comes onto the *arch*

*Carved
parallel turn*

of the foot. Here is where you begin loading the center of the ski to arc it into an edged, carved turn.

And as the arc begins to round out across the hill, scoot the skis forward just a bit to load the tails. This forward scoot shifts your weight onto the *heels* of your boots, pressing the tail of the skis solidly into the snow surface so the skis grip.

If the skis are going to skid, they're most likely to do so at the end of the turn, where centrifugal force and gravity both are pulling in the same direction. This can double or triple the force drawing you to the outside of the turn, so it's important to have the edge set solidly here. Slalom skis are engineered with stiff tails specifically to resist this end-of-turn loading and to provide solid edge grip where you need it most. But such a ski requires an athletic loading and un-loading of the tail. And you do it with this ball-of-foot entry, arch-of-foot middle and heel-of-foot exit from the turn.

4
MOGULS

SMOOTH
CONTROL IN
JAGGED
BUMPS

As a ski instructor, the question I get most frequently from advanced skiers is, "How can I ski in control in the bumps?" It's obvious that bumps can be fun. The best skiers grin all the way down the hairiest of mogul fields. But rational adults usually avoid moguls because they look like hard work. Skied fast, bumps can rattle your fillings loose. And they throw you in the air, where you may lose control and crash.

That flight through the air tells us what's wrong with the way a lot of folks approach moguls. Most skiers are taught to ski with an up-unweight technique. Instructors love to tell students to stand up tall to start the turn, a position that flattens and lightens the ski so it's easier to change edges. But every mogul-top is a little ski jump, so if you try to stand up straight there, you'll take off. Go fast, stand tall, and you'll be launched into the next county. With your skis in the air, you have very little opportunity to brake or turn. So you lose control.

Back off a bit. Approach mogul skiing first as an exercise in speed control, then as a way to perfect the terrain-unweighting skills discussed in Chapter Two.

G R E E N

SPEED CONTROL

Learning to ski bumps is a lot like practicing the piano: take it slow and easy so you hit the right notes. When we got to scary scales in F#, my piano teacher said, "Don't be afraid of the black keys. They're your friends. They tell you where you are on the keyboard." Likewise, the bumps can be your friends. They show you where to turn, and they'll help you start each turn if you let them do the unweighting.

But the first step will be to ski bumps slowly and carefully, so as not to get thrown. In any skiing situation, we brake by turning; so if we brake on every bump, our speed won't get out of hand. We'll start by turning to a complete stop at the top of each bump.

Stop at the top of a mogul field, and look downhill eight or ten feet to the first bump you'll come to. Decide which way you're going to turn when you get to that bump. Let's assume you'll turn right. That means you'll make a left turn to get down to the bump. And it will be a smooth, skidded, braking turn.

Start the left turn and slide the tails evenly, steering your ski tips toward the bump. As you near the bump, sink low into your fully-edged traverse position. At the same time, bring your right pole forward and point it at the top of the bump. Plant the pole just as you sink to a stop at the crest of the mogul.

*Speed control
exercise in bumps:
Turn to a stop on
each bump, planting
the pole as you stop.*

Now you're halted at the top of the bump, with pole planted, ankles and knees flexed, eyes focused downhill. Pick out the next bump you plan to use, one mogul farther downhill. Feel your skis. The tip and tail are off the snow because you're standing on top of a bump; it's very easy to pivot or steer your tips downhill, to start a new turn. As you steer the skis into the turn, you've changed edges—now you begin to slide down the back of the bump.

Steer your skis to the right, and get the tails skidding in another smooth braking motion. As the skid begins, bring the left pole forward and aim for a turn-to-stop on the top of bump number two, with the left pole planted.

Go from bump top to bump top, stopping on each mogul top, until you begin to develop a rhythm. When the pole plant comes smoothly with the stop, and the edge change and swivel go together smoothly to start the turn, it's time to upscale to a smooth, slow, flowing motion over the top of the bump—just eliminate the full stop. Link three or four slow turns. Then link five or six, then ten or twelve.

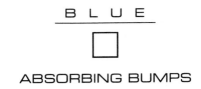

B L U E

ABSORBING BUMPS

As your rhythm improves, pick up speed. With more speed, there's more potential for the bumps to throw your skis into the air, so it's time to start "swallowing" the bump with a smooth ankle and knee flex.

Just for practice, make three or four full-stop mogul turns. As your tips rise to the top of a bump, flex the ankles and knees so that you arrive at the crest (and plant the pole) in an exaggeratedly retracted position.

Swallow the bump.

Steering into the new turn, straighten your legs to press your ski edges against the steep downhill side of the bump. In effect, you are standing tall as your skis slide into the trough and as you skid off speed. Here comes the next bump. Aim your pole for the crown, flex your ankles and knees, swallow the bump, and when the skis get light across the top, change edges and steer into the following trough.

As you adjust to the rhythm and flow of the moguls, pick up the pace. A little more speed means the skis will get lighter on the bump tops, and you should be able to back off the exaggerated absorption. Incidentally, the French word *avalement,* which refers to a turn made by absorbing terrain with ankles and knees, literally means swallowing (from the verb *avaler*). But for skiers, the word has a double meaning: *aval* means "downstream," or "toward the valley," so an avalement turn both swallows the bump and turns the skis downhill.

B L A C K

SHOVEL CONTACT

The average slalom ski has a carved-turn radius of about 40 meters, or approximately 130 feet. But the average mogul is only about 10 feet across. Obviously, we can't fit a pure carved turn, with its full-length edge contact, into the arc of a trough.

Instead, a mogul turn works mainly because the full edge of the ski doesn't lie on the snow, not in the beginning of the turn, anyway. Rather, as you crest the top of the bump, the tip rises, and continues to rise, blasting into the thin air beyond. When your feet meet the crest of the bump, it's time

(Continued on page 54)

Push the shovels down.

to press the shovel (the front half of the ski) onto the snow again for the beginning of a new turn.

Pressing the shovel down lifts the tail into the air—and lets you complete a short turn carved only on a third of the ski's length. The tail stays clear, preventing a hang-up against the walls of the trough.

As you ski the bumps slowly, think about maintaining full contact between the shovel and the snow. Let the shovel get light as you meet the bump by standing on the arch of your foot. Then increase pressure on the ball of the foot as you come over the top, and especially as you change edges. Push the front of the ski down the back of the bump to get good carving pressure between the ski edge and the steep backside of the mogul.

It takes quick feet, but this is how the experts maintain full-time, smooth control in bumps: by making the shovel carve on the snow all the way through the turn.

5
POWDER

Skiing powder is pure weightless pleasure, the most sensuous way to ski. It's so desirable that some people spend thousands of dollars riding helicopters to get to bottomless, untracked snow. To the expert powder skier, deep snow is really effortless, a gravity-powered float in space.

Ironic, then, how the new powder skier finds the stuff intimidating, frustrating and exhausting . . . To the beginner, powder seems to trap the skis. It hides them. When you crank your best hard-snow turn, powder trips you. Then it sits on your chest, so it's a wrestle just to get back on your feet.

Powder skiing is unlike hard-snow skiing in a number of ways, but much of the physics boils down to this: you need speed. Powder skiing is akin to water-skiing: forward speed is necessary so the skis will plane. In a few inches of new snow, where you can ski the firm surface underneath, all the powder does is smooth out the terrain, making turns flow like ripples of water. But in deep powder, the only way to get skis to turn is to maintain enough speed to float them.

Keep your speed up in powder so that skis will plane

This is why it's better to learn powder skiing on wide, soft, shorter skis—the more the ski looks like a water ski, the more easily it will float in deep snow. A ski that makes a broad platform planes at a lower, more comfortable speed. This is the reason for the continued popularity of weird fat skis like the Miller Soft, Atomic Powder Plus and RD Heli-dog; even of defunct models like the Rossignol Haute Route, RD Heliski and Molnar. If you're going into deep powder for the first time, things will go more smoothly if you beg, borrow or rent some wide floppy skis. Don't be proud. Leave your slalom boards at home and rent beginner skis if necessary.

Next, forget about racing turns, hard snow turns, skating turns. Forget any technique in which you stand against the outside ski. Put all your weight on one ski in powder, and it will simply sink to China, while the other (unweighted) ski bobs to the surface. Result: instant split, followed by tumble. Plan to stand on both skis equally, steering them together as if they were a single unit, like a surfboard or monoski. Think of your two skis as one broad plane arcing through the snow. It helps to keep the skis close together.

One thing you will retain from your hard-snow turn: a balanced stance. Stand in the middle of the ski, with ankles, knees and hips flexed slightly. Hands should be held wide and forward. Be loose and flexible. An emphatic unweighting motion, with an exaggerated pole plant, helps to lighten the skis for each new turn. In powder, rhythm is most important. Let the natural bounce rate of your skis determine the up-down, porpoising rhythm of your turns. It's almost like bouncing on a miniature trampoline.

G R E E N

FLIRT WITH THE FALL LINE

When you sink deep in powder, the weight and resistance of the snow quickly drags you to a stop. The only way to keep your skis moving, and planing, is to point your tips straight downhill. The deeper the snow, the more important it becomes to keep your skis running straight down the fall line. This sounds scary, but as soon as you experience how much easier it is to float into turns when the skis run faster, you'll see how exhilarating powder skiing can be.

Start easy. At the top of an open, unobstructed powder slope, stop and look down. Lift your downhill ski, point it straight toward the bottom of the bowl, and kick your ski tail back into the snow, with the tip pointing a bit above the horizontal. Stand on this platform, and do the same with the other ski, so that you're now standing still, on a solid, nearly level surface, facing straight downhill.

Now we're going to make a single half-turn, to the left. It's just a matter of pushing off with the poles and letting the skis glide straight downhill for a moment, until you feel them begin to lift and plane in the snow. As soon as the skis feel light and maneuverable, plant the left pole and bank the skis to the left.

The skis will start to turn. Don't force anything, but simply ride the turn all the way around to a stop. The stop will come quickly, because as the skis slow you'll sink deeper, like a water-skier letting go the rope. Try this half-turn to a stop again, this time to the right, and practice until you feel comfortable with the skis gliding in the fall line. Extend the glide phase for more speed if the skis still feel awkward.

Now begin a straight downhill glide and bounce gently on the skis. Feel how the skis float to the surface on each bounce. Add a pole plant to each bounce, and then a gentle

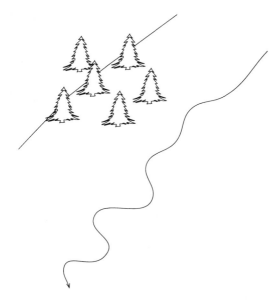

In powder, run straight until skis reach planing speed, then begin turns.

banking of the skis. Very quickly, the bounces become turns. In order to keep your speed up, though, don't really complete the turns—the skis never divert very far from the fall line. If they do, speed decays very quickly and you come to a quick stop.

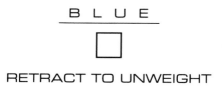

B L U E

RETRACT TO UNWEIGHT

Once you can make turns by bouncing your skis down a wide, smooth powder slope, begin to understand what your skis are actually doing down there, under the surface. When you straighten your legs, you drive the skis deeper and bow them into a turning arc. When you begin to flex your legs, it relieves pressure on the skis, helping them to float to the surface so you can steer into a new turn. In a way, this is much like the action used in smooth mogul skiing: extend the legs to pressure and carve the skis, and flex the legs to let the skis rise and steer.

With this in mind, make a powder run by retracting the legs (like tucking up your landing gear) to start each turn. I like to think of my skis as porpoising through the snow, as if they were following an invisible wave under the surface. Each time the skis come up for air, a new turn begins and the skis cross the fall line; then the skis plunge deep to point down the fall line again, arcing through the turn.

The retraction turn is especially useful in bottomless snow and when the snow is heavy or resistant, because it allows you to surface the skis at will. Just tuck your heels up under your bottom and the skis come along happily, ready to turn.

Extension-retraction-extension turn in powder

B L A C K

STEEPS AND TREES

When the terrain gets tight, with narrow steep gulleys and lots of trees to make rigid slalom gates, a short retraction powder turn will keep you away from the rocks and woods. In this environment, the ability to cleave to the fall line needs to be tempered by the ability to honk a short traverse around the impassable rock or tree without losing speed.

The problem most skiers run into when they crank a hard turn in powder is that turning away from the fall line slows you down while at the same time forcing your skis deeper into the snow. It's all too easy to overdo it and crunch to a halt. Sometimes the stop is so abrupt that you wind up vaulting over your skis in a high-siding crash.

Avoid the alarm-stop syndrome in three ways:

▲ First, plan your line two or three turns ahead. Keep your head up and read the surface of the snow and the tree tops for openings. Remember that you're not skiing trees; you're skiing the snow between the trees, and watch the white, not the green. Because we tend to move in the direction we look, if you focus on the trees (or rocks) you'll eventually ski straight into one. So, eyes on the snow.

▲ Second, use deeper pillows of snow for help in speed control. Instead of turning away from the fall line when you begin to move too fast, put your ski tips into the deeper drifts in the gulleys and on the lee sides of trees. In deep woods, especially on lower slopes where the surface is protected from the wind, snow often falls out of treetops to leave round, soft hummocks on the sur

Ski the fall line in trees.

face; when covered by a more recent storm, they look like big, friendly, isolated moguls. Your skis will run right through them, and slow you down comfortably in the process. These pillows are great fun. By using the terrain creatively, you can stay out of trouble without cranking far from the fall line.

▲ Finally, when you must finish a turn with a short traverse, keep speed up by immediately retracting the legs to float your skis to the surface, and head down the fall line again as soon as it's safe.

6
ICE

FEATHER THE EDGE

Skiers tend to regard skiing ice as the precise opposite of skiing powder: A loud and jarring experience that accelerates you toward the parking lot rather than controls your speed, and requires you to stand on one ski, not two. Yet the same rules of balance and timing pertain to ice as to any kind of snow. Accomplished ice skiers take the same pleasure in carving a smooth turn across boilerplate ice as does a hockey player.

The crucial skill is slicing the ski edge smoothly into a hard surface, and holding it there—smoothly—so it won't rattle loose. The smooth part is critical. Not even the strongest skier can use a ski edge like a hatchet, smashing it onto the ice hard enough to hold; a slammed edge will simply bounce off the surface. The trick is to carve the edge gently into the ice; think of the ski edge as a scissors blade, not a meat cleaver. The scissors blade meets the paper at a subtle angle and works through mechanical advantage, not brute impact energy. So you need to stay balanced, to feather the ski gently onto its edge and feather off again when G-forces late in the turn begin to overpower the holding capacity of the ice and edge.

Remember this about skiing ice: nothing works well unless your ski edges are reasonably sharp, and polished smooth. Where ice is a common ski area condition, experts tune their skis every day, even if all that means is just polishing the edges with a fine whetstone in the morning. If you ski ice, it's a fine idea to carry a pocket whetstone in your parka, and learn to use it.

G R E E N

STABLE PATIENCE TURNS

First of all, ice is no cause for panic. There's ice and there's *ice*. . . . Most of the time you can simply avoid the worst of the blue and yellow water ice and ski on toothier, more edgeable white ice. When I lived in New York and had to ski ice in New England, often I could skirt the shiny patches, or simply ski straight across them and make my turns on the duller-looking edgeable stuff.

But let's assume for a moment that you're looking down a consistently armorplated ski run, bulletproof from top to bottom and side to side. You can get down alive, and even with pride, if you keep your skis under you and don't get going too terribly sideways. The secret is balance. Remember the balanced, athletic stance from Chapter One? Let's review, quickly: feet about hip-width apart, weight on the arches; ankles, knees and hips flexed slightly, with a neutral stance in your boots; hands up and in front, back bent naturally, eyes focused down the hill.

In this position you could glide sideways and at a fairly good clip without falling down. Skiers who get into trouble on ice are the ones who lean uphill, rotating wildly in the direction they think is safe. Actually what they're doing is pushing their own skis out from under them in the downhill direction. Maintain the balanced, athletic stance and ice loses most of its terror.

In this stance, start your turn very gently. Now, if you had to cross a skating rink in your bedroom slippers, you'd try to avoid any sudden movement that could break traction, and the same is true with skis on ice. Abrupt motion leads to a skid. Begin the turn slowly, and let it develop naturally, following the arc of the ski. This should be a turn without muscle: a patience turn.

Fortunately, it's very easy to steer on ice—there's almost no resistance to steering the skis through the fall line. Once established, the turn finishes pretty quickly. And almost at once, you'll feel the tails of the skis begin to skid sideways on the ice. Hold that skid just long enough to lose a little speed, but don't force it. Instead, cross your body over the skis, chest and shoulders headed downhill to begin another turn. It's safer to start a new turn, gently, than to force the old turn into a badly skidded, accelerating traverse.

Because the ice makes steering so easy, the turn can start with an oh-so-subtle motion. Just the smallest unweighting or crossover motion is enough to end the old turn and begin the skis moving in a new direction. So you may not feel 100 percent in control—on glare ice, no one does—but you can be smooth, balanced and safe.

(*Continued on page 69*)

The balanced parallel turn helps you stay upright and in control on ice, even in a skid.

B L U E

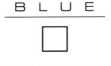

LOADING ONE SKI

Once you have established a rhythmic series of smooth patience turns and are happy with your balance, it's time to arc the ski a little to make it bite a bit better. Do this by putting all the weight on the outside ski. Concentrating all your weight in the center of one ski gets you a more solid edgeset with that ski.

Start your patience turn. As the skis pass through the fall line, think about settling your weight onto the outside ski and lift the tip of the inside ski just an inch off the snow.

For more edging power, unload the inside ski to drive the outside ski solidly.

Hold the turn, standing on the heel of your downhill foot, until it finishes out. Then put the inside ski tip down and begin a new turn.

You lift the tip of the inside ski, and not the tail, in order to move your balance point back just an inch, from the arch to the heel of the outside boot. This gives a stronger load path to the edge of the ski, and drives the stiffest, narrowest part of the ski, its tail, into engagement with the ice. Right away, you should feel less skidding at the end of the turn, so you can hold your patience turn a bit longer.

When you feel comfortable standing on one ski, and on your heel at that, experiment with edge angle. Roll the ski up onto a slightly higher edge by moving the knee uphill, very subtly. If the ski really carves into the ice, this higher edge angle will tighten the turn.

As soon as the ski begins to skid, though, put your inside ski down and roll into a new turn. Don't try to save a turn that's already decayed into a skid. It's almost impossible to end a skid on ice, so get the new turn started.

B L A C K

SKATING ON ICE

The best ice skiers are ice skaters. Whether figure skaters or hockey players, they learned long ago to move smoothly from one foot to the other, and how to balance on a single slicing edge. If you can happily hold an edge on one ski from the fall line to the end of the turn, you too can learn to skate onto the new ski. Doing a smooth skating step gets the edge of the new ski carving earlier, and makes a more efficient turn.

The expert finishes a high-speed carved turn on ice with a diverging step.

Remember that the weight shift movement has to be subtle on ice. So instead of standing up onto the new uphill ski, make a smooth, rolling, lateral motion in the direction of the new turn. Visualize the way a speed skater moves on the ice—there's no wasted vertical motion of the upper body. All the energy is directed across the blade and in the direction of travel.

You're finishing the turn, weight on the outside ski. Before the skid develops, plant your pole (gently!) and smoothly move the shoulders downhill. This has the effect, immediately, of rolling the skis onto their new edges, so steer them, simultaneously, into the new turn. And immediately, begin to lift the new inside ski just half an inch off the ice to get your weight loading smoothly onto the new outside ski. Use knee angulation to control the radius of the turn.

7
STEEP

COOPERATE
WITH GRAVITY

For most recreational skiers, the whole point of improving skill level is to be able to ski comfortably on progressively steeper terrain. The important word here is comfortably. What appears steep and scary to Joe Green can look fun and challenging to Suzy Blue and downright old-shoe easy to Stan Black. Every skier has a comfort level. Challenge that sense of ease, and you feel the need for steep skiing skills, regardless of the actual, measured slope angle.

An important concept to understand here is that no one has ever conquered gravity. To all intents and purposes, gravity is the Universe, Fate, God's Will, and City Hall—you can't fight it and win. You can rail against gravity, but you're better off just enjoying it. The secret is in massaging gravity, in finessing and co-opting it. To get along, as Sam Rayburn said, you've got to go along. The expert skier uses gravity as an empowerment, and gets a free ride. The fool gets a beating.

This may not be of much help to the frightened skier trying to imagine how he's going to live through the next ten yards of elevator shaft. So let's back off for a second and consider the simple "survival sideslip."

G R E E N

THE SAFE SIDESLIP

Beginning with the notion that it's safer to descend in control, feet first and on your skis, than out of control, headfirst and on your back, the smart way to handle any slope too steep for comfort is in a balanced sideslip.

Once again we're back to the balanced athletic stance from Chapter One. Skis need to be comfortably apart (on steep terrain, they'll have to be wider, simply because your uphill ski is farther above your downhill ski). Weight is on the arch of your foot; ankles, knees, hips and back are flexed; hands are out front and eyes focused downhill. In this position, and with the skis across the hill, a controlled downhill sideslip is easy to do. Just roll both knees away from the hill slightly, and gravity will do the rest.

The trick is to get the tip and tail of the ski sliding sideways together, at the same speed, so the slip doesn't develop into a screaming forward (or backward!) plunge. If the tails begin to slide faster, lean forward a bit; if the tips slide faster, push on the tails. A little experimenting will teach you very quickly exactly where to stand on the skis for a smooth, controlled sideslip.

Control your speed with edge angle, by rolling the knees smoothly. Stop by driving the edge with an uphill knee motion. Do this with the knees only; (if you bank the upper body into the hill, you'll lose your balance, the ski edges will unlock from the snow, and you'll slide the rest of the way on your butt). As soon as you're off the steep part, the sideslip

Balanced sideslip on steep

can be converted smoothly into a traverse or a turn, and you're off and running on more comfortable terrain.

B L U E

REACH DOWNHILL

Back to basic principles again. Remember that speed is controlled with the end of the turn, when the skis begin to track across the hill. Acceleration happens during the first half of the turn, when the skis begin to seek the fall line. Turning safely on steep terrain should, logically, be a matter of getting the first half of the turn done quickly, so we can get to the important part of the turn—the braking.

Gravity can help here. Gravity will pull you into and through the first half of the turn easily, if you'll let it. What works, of course, is to move with gravity; in this case, to project the upper body downhill to start the new turn. It

Reach downhill for the pole plant.

takes faith in yourself, faith that your legs will follow, catch up and get back under you in time to start braking.

The key to a confident turn on the steeps is in the pole plant. Simply reach far downhill to plant the pole. This reaching motion commits the shoulders and chest to the turn early, and starts the skis steering into the fall line promptly. At the same time, the pole plant gives you a point of stability, a reassuring anchor on which to hang the turn.

Here's how to do it. At the top of a smooth, steep pitch, assume your athletic stance: weight square in the center of your downhill ski, shoulders and eyes aimed downhill. As you glide forward in a traverse, reach as far downhill as you can with the downhill pole, then lean farther out to plant it.

Bang. With the pole plant, the turn has started. Now simply keep your shoulders, chest and eyes focused downhill and smoothly bring the legs around, settling onto the new outside ski, and turn to a stop. Have your new outside pole ready for a down-reaching pole plant, and try to turn again in the other direction. When you feel comfortable with this turn-to-a-stop, eliminate the stop and make a rhythmic series of reach-down turns.

B L A C K

RELEASE THE DOWNHILL KNEE

Super steep terrain (upwards of 40 degrees in pitch) doesn't hold snow very well. Any turn has the potential to kick the loose snow off in a slough or miniature avalanche. What you're really looking for is good edge grip on the firmer surface underneath the new, loose snow.

One-two-three turn

At this angle, we've moved into the realm of the extreme skier, and we need a bombproof turn, a turn that will produce a solid edgeset every time, regardless of snow conditions. In narrow couloirs, the top extreme skiers use a turn I call the one-two-three: one for the pole plant, two for the downhill ski and three for the uphill ski.

Here's how it works. From a solid traverse position, look downhill at the point where you expect your skis to land on the next turn. The following should happen quickly, as quickly as you can clap your hands three times. *One:* reach down hill and plant the pole. *Two:* release the downhill ski by pointing the downhill knee into the new turn. *Three:* follow with the uphill ski, swinging through to land on it in the new traverse position.

In dangerous narrow couloirs and on avalanche tracks, ski the one-two-three turn to a stop each time, so you can test the stability of the snow before committing to the next turn.

8
CRUD AND CRUST

T U R N   W H E N
S K I S   A R E
S T U C K

The heavy, wet, sticky goop left on the mountainside by a warm blizzard is often called Sierra cement, though it appears on any mountain range close to an ocean or large lake. California's Sierra have no patent on wet snow. Powder can be even soggier in the Pacific Northwest and in the lake-effect counties of the Midwest and upstate New York. After it's been stirred around for a few hours by eager-beaver skiers, heavy powder turns into an inconsistent muck, full of heavy globules that can deflect a ski from its intended course. The worst crud snow can have the viscosity of peanut butter, chunky style.

The big problem with skiing this stuff is the way it seems to trap the skis. No skier born has the strength to pivot a ski sideways in heavy junk; the bindings will release before you can force such a steered turn. This leaves us with two options in crud: the pure carved turn, with its long radius and concomittant high speed; or some aggressive unweighting motion meant to unstick skis from the glue.

The other common snow condition that traps skis irretrievably is crust. Powder bowls develop a thin dense suncrust after baking for a few days under a cloudless sky. More difficult to manage is windslab, a thick and durable crust compacted on the surface by continuous high winds. When your skis get trapped under a crust, you have to be very strong, very balanced and very lucky to keep moving and ski in control.

G R E E N

KICK TURN

The inexperienced skier trapped at the top of some muck-covered hilltop may have only one safe option: the Z-turn descent. Z turning is a series of traverses punctuated by kick turns. The kick turn is an awkward-looking but efficient way to reverse direction without actually moving from a secure spot. It's about the only safe way to turn your skis around while standing still on a steep or difficult slope. The most famous kick turner of them all is Sandra Poulsen who, at Squaw Valley in 1948, used 22 of them to descend a steep peak, now officially named KT-22 in her honor.

So the kick turn has a long, honorable, though modest history. It may be an admission of defeat ("NO WAY am I going to point my skis downhill here, buster"), but it's a handy device nonetheless. Ski instructors use the kick turn all the time in pivoting to address a class and then reversing to ski away.

Here's how to do it: Start in your traverse position, at a standstill but with shoulders turned to face downhill. Put both poles in the snow on your uphill side and lean on them lightly for stability. Now lift your downhill foot high, straight

(Continued on page 84)

Kick turn

ahead, until the ski is more or less vertical and the tail of the
ski rests on the snow. Pivot that foot and ski around to point
in the opposite direction to the uphill ski. With both skis on

the snow again, you'll find your feet in the classic Charlie Chaplin pose—one points east and the other points west. If it feels more graceful to think of this as a *plié,* please do so.

Finally, stand on the downhill ski, lift the uphill ski and swing it around to the downhill side. Now the skis are re-united and, your poise restored, you are ready to traverse off through the muck to the other side of the slope, losing a few yards of elevation in the process. When you reach the tree line yonder, stop and repeat the process. If you're lucky, you can get down in fewer than 22 kick turns.

B L U E

LEAPERS

In one sense, crud and crust creates the same problem you face in very steep terrain: you know how to finish the turn, but getting started with your skis trapped is another matter altogether. Difficulties are complicated by deep junk, though, because you can't depend on gravity to get the turn started. You have to muscle the skis out by yourself.

A leaper turn is simply a powerful up-unweight. As you finish the turn into the traverse position, sink low on your skis, then combine a solid pole plant with an aggressive leap upward. (If accomplished at moderate speed, the leaper usu-ally clears the skis from the snow. As they break free, simply steer the skis down the fall line.) Land in balance, with weight equally distributed between the two skis and fore-and-aft. Bank against the skis just as you do in powder and let the skis arc under the surface to finish the turn.

You can practice the leaper turn on smooth, groomed terrain before heading for the deep muck. But the turn re-quires so much energy, and a long run of leapers produces so much sweat, that I reserve it for emergencies, situations in which the snow is truly unskiable by other means.

Leaper turn

If you're light and can ski gently, the leaper may not be necessary on thick windslab snow. There, the skier with a subtle feel for the snow may be able to stay on the surface. It's great fun to stay on top, brushing the skis lightly over the dry, edgeable surface, while heavier, clumsier skiers sink through and have to resort to leaps and curses. This is a good example of expert relativity. The smoothest or fastest skier in any given crowd is by definition the expert. Another way to put it is that it's a lot more fun to see your friends crash than to crash yourself.

B L A C K

FALL-LINE FLOATERS

After you've had some experience in wet junk, you'll gradually develop a feel for just how much leap to use in a leaper turn. When you can consistently bring the skis just to the surface, and turn them there instead of in the air, you're ready to adapt the deep powder retraction turn to crud.

Because heavy snow offers so much more resistance than bottomless airy powder, you don't get nearly as much decambering when you pressure the skis. This means that the turn radius in junk tends to be longer and the speed higher. If you're comfortable at GS speeds—20 to 45 mph—you'll find junk snow easier to ski simply because there's more kinetic energy available. You can substitute a subtle extension-retraction motion for the leaper.

To the extent that this is a pure carved turn, depending on the ski's sidecut radius to establish the arc of the turn, it's a patience turn—you have to wait for the ski to finish the turn for you. But once the turn is finished and the skis are arrowing across the bowl again, match your pole plant with a

GS-floater turn

strong leg-retraction/edge change. The skis will come easily near the surface and arc toward the fall line. Because you don't actually have to get the skis in the air to change edges, this turn works pretty smoothly even in moderately crusted snow.

An equipment note is in order. Heavy snow is easiest to ski using stable aluminum GS skis, for two reasons. First, a solid, stable ski bounces around less as you track through inconsistent, cut-up crud; the skis are simply smoother and easier to balance on. Second, aluminum skis are built for good gliding speed in wet snow. They vibrate like tuning forks, breaking up the water layer under the base into microscopic droplets. The result is that the ski glides easily from dry snow (in the shadows) into wet snow (in the sun) without decelerating. Once again, the advantage is that the ski is more predictable and easier to balance upon.

The corollary to all this is that a good slick wax job is most important when the snow is carved up and inconsistent. The difference between a dry, sticky base and a properly waxed base is like the difference between steel wheels and polyurethane wheels on a skateboard. A dry base will eventually trip you up; a waxed base can slip you through in stylish control.

9
TREES

Sheltered from the wind and sun, powder remains deeper, smoother and longer in the woods. Expert skiers love tree skiing, and accept the many real dangers as the price of immediate pleasures.

For a number of reasons, it's best not to ski in the trees alone. It's easy to get lost in the woods, and even easier to get hurt either by colliding with a tree or falling in a tree well. Even a minor injury becomes serious when you're all alone, moving slowly, with night coming on quickly. In fact, it's safest to ski in groups of three or more, so that if a person is hurt, one skier can stay with the injured party while another goes for help. Every member of the group should have an avalanche transceiver and understand how to use it; a couple of members should carry snow shovels.

G R E E N

FOCUS ON THE WHITE

The inexperienced skier should stay out of the woods, at least until achieving some level of expertise in powder skiing (see Chapter Five). But many ski resorts provide "gladed" areas where the trees have been thinned, and these are good places to practice powder skills.

In any sport, the body tends to move where the eye leads. Prove this to yourself while cycling or even driving. If you focus the eyes on the right side of the road, the vehicle drifts in that direction. To the same effect in tennis and baseball, you need to keep your eye on the ball to meet it with the bat. In tree skiing there's a strong temptation to look at the trees.

To ski the woods safely, focus on the snow, not on the trees.

Avoid this, because it will eventually lead you into a tree. Instead, focus on the white stuff between the trees. Concentrate on where you want to ski, not on where you want to avoid.

Beyond that, relax and use your bounce-bounce-bounce technique. Just keep your skis as close to the fall line as the forest will allow, and bounce against your skis rhythmically. As the skis lighten between bounces they float to the surface. This is the moment to steer them into the new turn. Use the heavily loaded, arced-ski down-bounce portion of the cycle to complete the turn.

Days after the last storm has passed, snow in the glades will pack down under skier traffic and come to resemble a mogul field. The difference is that each mogul has a tree growing from its crest. Obviously, you can't simply pivot your turns on top of the bumps; you've got to follow the troughs. It's almost like following the ruts in a race course, except that collision with the gates can cause worse than bruises.

In this environment, remember the speed control exercise in Chapter Four: ski nearly to a stop above each tree, then steer your skis down into the next trough to start a new turn. If you skid off speed before each mogul, you can maintain good control all the way to the bottom of the glade.

B L U E

RECOVER IN THE FALL LINE

If you've mastered powder skiing in open bowls, the only problem you'll encounter in the woods is staying in the fall line. In the woods, you'll frequently zip around a small stand of trees and find another big one blocking your line. This calls for a quick decision. Right or left?

The safe route is usually the one closest to the fall line, even if that looks like the steeper drop. The reason is that a hard turn to a traverse loads the skis and buries them deep. In powder this is the best way to court a tumble, and if you do it close above a tree well the energy of your stop can easily collapse the snow wall, dropping you into the well.

Turn instead in a direction that will put your next turn into the fall line. You can afford to crank a good one if you maintain enough momentum to get the skis pointing back downhill. Once in the fall line, speed will float your skis toward the surface and let you get sorted out, centered and ready for action again.

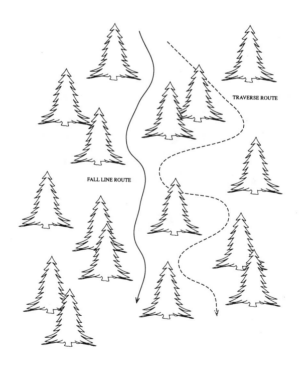

Safe route in tree-skiing is usually the fall line.

Watch the experts in powder. Good skiers consistently seek the most direct fall-line route. Whenever a hot powder skier gets in trouble, he recovers by regaining planing speed in the fall line.

B L A C K

BALANCE FOR THE UNEXPECTED

The woods are natural terrain, untouched by the bulldozer except for the odd traverse road. The trees hide a wonderful variety of cliffs, boulders, sinkholes and, yes, road cuts. Inevitably, the demon tree skier, hewing to the fall line, bursts blindly between close-set hemlocks to sail off the edge of the world.

Balance in the air

Ski the trees in balance at all times, in the certain knowl-
edge that you'll be airborne for at least a few feet sometime
in the course of the day. Powder landings are soft and cush-
iony, so if you land on the middle of your skis you can
usually ski away, giggling.

To land centered, you have to launch centered. If you ski
powder by leaning back on the stiff tails of your slalom skis,
air time will see you rotating farther back, to land staring at
the sky. Landing on the tails of your skis always holds the
risk of knee injury. So keep the hands forward when skiing
tight trees. As in the race course, this will keep you centered
on the skis. And you can always use your gloves to clear the
branches from in front of your face.

10
SLUSH

BALANCE IN INCONSISTENT SNOW

Springtime brings long sunny days, acres of spectacular easy-to-ski corn snow . . . and sticky accumulations of slush. Slush by itself may be grabby and slow, but if that's all there were to it you could ski it with the same patience turns you'd use in junk and crud. The real problem with slush is that it lives alongside ice. You get tripped up skiing over a fast, skittery patch of ice (in the shade) into a treacly puddle of slush (in the sun) and back again onto ice. As skis hit the slush, they decelerate, throwing the unprepared skier forward. Just as you've about adjusted to the slush, out you pop onto ice, where your skis want to skid sideways.

G R E E N

WAX FOR GLIDE

No one glides easily through slush without properly waxed skis. When the snow is mostly water, the ski base creates lots of suction which resists every motion of the ski. Caught in slush, a dry ski base sticks when you try to glide, steer or skid. About all you can do easily is edge.

The solution, of course, is a daily coat of wax. When you wax your car or kitchen floor, water beads on the shiny surface. Wax on the base of a ski serves the same function: it makes a sheet of water bead up into tiny droplets. These droplets function as ball bearings, and the ski in fact rolls on them. The air between the ball bearings is roughly 100 times

Sun-warned show alternates with shaded ice.

less viscous than the water. Naturally, if the wax is right and the meltwater beads up, the suction effect largely disappears.

Cold snow is dry, with a low water content. Waxing isn't quite as important here (though still necessary for maximum ski performance). Warm snow, near the melting point, is soggy. Wax becomes critical if you want to ski smoothly. While any wax is better than no wax, it's best to pick a wax appropriate to the snow temperature. Wax for warm, wet snow is softer and more water repellent than wax for cold, hard snow crystals. Most wax companies identify their soft warm-snow waxes with "warm" colors: yellow, orange or red; one or two smaller companies identify the warm-snow waxes with a silver pigment.

A versatile alternative is the modern fluorinated wax, an all-purpose preparation that gets its water repellency from chemical additives rather than from the soft wax. This is what I use on my own skis. Fluorinated waxes like Swix F4 and Hertel Hot Sauce work well in all snow conditions.

The proper way to apply most waxes is to iron the stuff into the base. But in the spring it's a good idea to carry a bar of the appropriate wax in your parka pocket. When the skis feel a bit sticky, rub wax on the bases.

Naturally, because of those icy spots, you'll also need clean, sharp edges. Keep your skis tuned and waxed, and the slush-ice phenomenon will harbor no snow snakes for you.

BLUE

READING THE SUN

Slush is soft. Ski it like deep snow, with weight evenly distributed between your two skis. Ice is hard. Ski it like a race course, weighting one ski at a time.

Moving from one style to another as the snow conditions change is one of the hallmarks of the versatile, experienced skier. You need to master both powder and ice techniques (see Chapters Five and Six) to ski well in inconsistent spring snow. Just as important, you need to read the surface of the snow ahead to gauge which technique to use as conditions change.

As you ski, be aware of the sun. Early in the morning, with the sun still low in the sky, most of the mountain will be pretty icy—yesterday's slush and corn has frozen overnight. It may be pretty rough ice, too, since yesterday's ski tracks in the slush will have frozen solid on many runs. Deploy your

Shade side can be dry or frozen; sunny side can be soft or slushy.

best ice-skating style, and treat the whole mountain as a race course.

By 10:00 A.M. slopes that face east will be getting pretty soft. Cat tracks, which are flat, will be inconsistent; soft in the bright sunny spots, still slick in the shade. As you ski past trees or around corners, be aware that dark areas will require weighting one ski at a time, while bright areas can be skied powder-style.

By noon, most of the mountain has softened up, and east-facing slopes, which have been baking all morning, may be ankle deep in slush. You'll find the best, most consistent skiing on contours that have been protected from the sun most of the day, perhaps on trails facing northwest. But be aware that some of the steeper trails facing north may get little or no sun even in late spring. These are the runs that hold snow long into the spring and, while they provide the best snow cover, they may also stay icy late into the day. They'll be the first to ice up in late afternoon, too.

As the sun drops toward the western horizon, the light goes flat on east-facing slopes, and they begin to firm up. Expect to encounter icy patches. You may want to head down the mountain via the sunlit western exposures.

BLACK

GS TURNS ON CORN

Next to powder, the most exhilarating type of snow is good spring corn. Corn is skier shorthand for melt/freeze granular snow. After a surface has baked in the sun and refrozen overnight, it melts again into little round pellets—like grains of corn. Depending on the temperature and the number of

GS turn on corn snow

melt/freeze cycles, corn can lie anywhere from half an inch to several inches deep.

Half an inch to an inch of corn makes smooth, effortless skiing. You can get an edge into the stuff, and it holds an arced turn beautifully. And there's a firm surface underneath, so the skis don't bog—nothing resists steering or skidding. In fact, the pellets behave like ball bearings, so skis glide like the wind. A smooth expanse of untracked corn snow is a ticket to high-speed heaven. Here is God's reason for inventing the pure carved giant slalom turn.

Where the corn is great, you can make all kinds of mistakes and get away scot-free. Corn is that forgiving. But always be aware that spring snow can be inconsistent. The quality and depth of the corn depends purely on its exposure to the sun, so it's always possible to go cooking into a shady area of ice or a solar-oven gulley where the snow sags like melting ice cream.

So stand centered, and be prepared for sudden changes in snow texture as you cross contours in the snow. On half an inch of corn, balance against one ski, but keep the other ski gliding along on the surface ready for equal-weighted action if you plunge into deep soup.

11
CHUTES

The skier who seeks out terrain challenges sooner or later will peer down some steep pitch that seems far too narrow for safe turns. It doesn't have to be a wild couloir (French for avalanche chute); it may simply be a place where a steep trail necks down between close-set rocks or trees.

If you're comfortable with fall-line skiing, you may feel happy descending a chute so narrow that the length of your skis would preclude standing across the thing in a traverse position. Most skiers are not this confident, especially when the price of blowing a turn may be a pinball ricochet off the rocky walls.

G R E E N

O

SLIP OUT OF TROUBLE

The only smart move for the new skier caught in a chute is to sideslip out (see Chapter Seven). Be aware that the snow in the bottom of a chute probably isn't smooth; more likely, you'll find yourself standing in a trough, the edges of the chute higher than the middle. This means that when you put your skis across the chute in a sideslip position, you'll be standing on the tips and tails; there's a good chance the centers of the skis will actually be off the snow. In a wider chute, you may find that short, steep moguls make full-length edge grip problematical.

If this is the case, sideslipping won't be a smooth operation. The edges may catch and skip unpredictably. Try to put

Sideslip on rough surfaces

all your weight on the downhill ski. This should bow it far enough to engage the center of the ski so the whole edge slides smoothly sideways. In moguls, sideslip down the convex steep side of each bump so your weight concentrates through the center of the ski, with tip and tail cantilevered over the troughs.

If that doesn't work, and if sideslipping feels too unstable, simply sidestep downward to smoother, safer terrain. It's just like walking downstairs sideways. Plant your poles solidly before taking each step, and make sure the edge of the ski will hold your weight before moving the other ski downward.

In a worst case situation (lousy weather, bad equipment, nasty snow) you may be tempted simply to take off your skis and walk down. When the snow is deep or icy, this is not advisable. In deep snow, without skis you might sink to the crotch; on ice, the steel edges of your skis provide much more secure purchase than the round plastic edges of your ski boot soles.

BLUE

ONE-TWO-THREE TURNS

This is as good a time as any to learn the short-radius, inside-knee turn, as practiced by extreme skiers when the going is really tough.

You already know that in steep terrain it's easiest to start the turn by leaning far downhill to make the pole plant. Technique in a chute requires that you relocate the skis to a point directly below the pole plant, without arcing a full medium-radius turn. You can't plant the pole and depend on a leisurely rollover to get your edges changed. Instead, you've

One-two-three turn

got to kick the skis loose from the snow right now and plant them down there.

One: From your traverse position, reach downhill and plant the pole. *Two:* Pick up your downhill ski. You are now standing on the uphill ski. *Three:* Push off your uphill ski into a jump; pivot around the planted pole and land on both skis together, in a traverse position.

Stop there and reconsider your position. Are you stable? How's the snow? Can you get away with another one-two-three turn? Always consider sideslipping for a bit—better to emerge upright than sliding on your back.

B L A C K

SKATEBOARD TURNS

The most fun you can have in a trough-shaped chute is banking your skis off the sloping snowy walls. It's the equivalent of what a skateboarder or snowboarder does in a half-pipe. To do this safely, the chute needs to be fairly commodious. A quick skier can get away with banked turns when the chute is perhaps 20 feet wide.

Simply ski up the side of the trough, carrying moderate speed. As gravity slows you, you'll feel the skis grow light. Steer your skis smoothly back toward the middle of the chute, gain speed and shoot up the opposite side for a repeat.

The real thrill in this turn is how effortless it quickly becomes. Going straight up the chute wall, you're balanced between gravity (pulling you back), momentum (pushing you up) and centrifugal force (holding you to the wall). You really don't need much edgeset or carving action going up the wall; the skis can be fairly flat against the snow surface. This means that when you reach that nearly weightless point

Skateboard turn on side of gully

at the top of your trajectory up the wall, you don't even need a crossover or edge change, just that smooth steering motion to keep the skis under you as gravity brings your body inevitably back to the middle of the chute.

With enough practice and more speed, a really quick skier can shoot a vertical line up the trough, retract the skis at the apex, pivot in the air around a pole plant, and dive straight back down his upward tracks. Slick.

12
VERSATILITY

READ THE SNOW AND ADAPT

The skiers I most admire are those who thoroughly enjoy every kind of snow and terrain. In powder or on ice, in moguls and on cornice-capped cliffs, they make balanced, rhythmic, controlled and exuberant turns. You never catch one of these skiers sitting in the lodge grousing about lousy snow or even lousy weather—they're out in it, having fun.

Attaining all-mountain, all-terrain mastery requires three elements. First, an attitude that you go up the mountain to have fun, not to work hard, and you may as well have fun often. Second, a solid sense of balance with a confident stance on the middle of the ski. And third, a willingness to adapt timing, stance and speed to the quality of the snow and shape of the terrain. A skier needs to be flexible, to read the snow and adapt to it.

Here are some simple exercises designed to help you move quickly from hard snow to soft snow styles.

G R E E N

O

WIDE STANCE TO NARROW

Intermediate students are frequently disappointed when I refuse to teach them how to ski with feet locked close together. Versatile, efficient skiing requires independent leg action, so you can snake across rugged terrain smoothly and in balance. The legs should act like the independent suspension on a sports car, not like an unstable pogo stick.

For most ski area trails, a comfortable stance with feet about hip-width apart works well. The distance between your boots provides plenty of clearance for knee angulation. When your weight goes to the outside ski as the turn develops, there's room to steer the inside ski and edge it lightly for use as the backup system or training wheel if your balance is upset on the outside ski.

In some situations, such as powered short turns on the race course and very steep terrain, you need a wider stance, to give more room for a steeper edge angle. In some situations (deep soft snow, tight moguls), you need a narrower stance, to weight the skis more equally and use them as a unit platform.

With the skis spaced about hip-width apart, make some rhythmic turns down a smooth intermediate trail. Start with a fairly long turn, and count off as if you were conducting a band: *turn* two three four, *turn* two three four (each *turn* can signal a pole plant). After eight or ten turns, shorten the count to *turn* two three, *turn* two three. After another eight or ten turns, shorten the count again: *turn* two, *turn* two, *turn* two, *turn* two.

Depending on the length and stiffness of your skis, one of these turning rhythms will feel easier and more natural than the others; a longer ski likes a longer turn; a livelier ski likes a shorter turn; and so on. When you've found a rhythm that feels free and easy, practice it until it comes naturally. Then go back to the top of the hill.

Now start another run, making that same rhythmic turn. After eight or ten turns, widen your stance about six inches and continue skiing. Does the rhythm change? Does the turn shape change? If you're like most skiers, you'll find that the wider stance puts your outside ski on a higher edge angle, producing a shorter, more powerful and more athletic turn.

After another eight or ten turns, bring the skis close together; not so close as to touch, but perhaps so your knees tough lightly. Keep skiing in rhythm. What happens to the turn? Usually, you get a little flatter edging angle, and a smoother, straighter, less energetic turn.

Go back to a normal stance, and repeat the exercise. You should feel comfortable changing from a wide to a narrow stance and back, and anticipate the changes that the changing stance will make in your turns and timing.

B L U E

ONE SKI, TWO SKI

Repeat the wide stance/narrow stance exercise (the Green exercise in this chapter), but use a longer, faster turn. When you move to a wider stance, try picking the inside ski right up off the snow. Angle the outside knee down a bit to get a more aggressive edgeset, and feel the ski power around in a solid GS turn. When you balance against the thin edge of the outside ski, you'll find that extra speed helps, just as speed helps you balance more solidly on a bicycle.

Now go back to your normal stance, and make the transition to a feet-together position with weight evenly split

*One-ski turn
with independent legs*

between the two skis. Notice that the turn becomes
smoother, floatier, less aggressive. Practice making the tran
sition from standing against one ski to floating along on two,
and back again. The first wide-set technique is a high-

Two-ski turn, weight on both feet

performance turn for racing and icy snow. The second is an
efficient way to ski in deep snow.

On a powder day, find a smooth groomed trail with a field
of deep new snow alongside. Make half a dozen high-

performance, one-footed turns on the groomed snow and then, with the feet evenly weighted, dive into the deep snow and make a half dozen bouncing powder turns, feet working as a platform. Loop out onto the groomed terrain and go back to your skated, one-foot-at-a-time racing turn. Back into the powder. Repeat the exercise until you feel comfortable switching between the two surfaces and the two techniques at will.

BLACK

PRESSURE VARIATIONS

Begin a series of rhythmic, medium-radius or giant slalom turns on a smooth intermediate trail. On each turn, stand solidly on the arch of your foot, your shin pressing lightly against the tongue of the boot.

After about eight turns, begin to scoot the outside ski forward just a little bit, so that your weight comes down on your heel as the pressure builds toward the end of the turn. What happens to the ski? The edge may bite a little harder, and the turn will tighten on skis with relatively stiff tails (aggressive slalom skis, for example). With other skis, the tips may grow light and unstable.

After a few turns, go back to standing on the arch of the foot. Which style feels better on your skis?

Now lean forward a bit, putting pressure on the ball of the foot. Flex your ankle to press the shin against the tongue of the boot. Now you're loading the shovel of the ski instead of the tail or center. What happens to the ski? On many skis, the tail will grow light and may skid smoothly outward, tightening the turn and braking off speed.

Go back to a centered stance, weight on the arch, and see if you can change the pressure on the sole of the foot throughout the length of the turn. As you cross over and project the upper body downhill in starting the turn, let the pressure build on the ball of your foot. As the skis approach the fall line, move back a hair to stand against the arch of the foot. As you round out into the end of the turn, scoot the outside foot forward so you finish the turn with weight solidly on the heel. Experiment with the timing of these weight shifts and find a smooth transition that seems to suit the design and flex of your skis.

Conduct the same series of experiments on hard snow, then in deep snow. Train your feet to find the middle of the ski for each different condition. Because skis equally weighted in powder often don't bow into the same arc as a fully-weighted single ski on hard snow, you may be able to stay more centered in deep snow. On ice, it often helps to move quickly to the heel in order to take advantage of the extra holding power of the stiff tail.

On groomed terrain, make a series of rhythmic up-unweighted turns. Now snake a series of extension-retraction or down-unweighted turns: retract the legs as they cross under your body, and extend them out to the sides as they head for the fall line. This is a smooth, snaky way to ski. The upper body moves in a straight, direct line downhill, without the bobbing motion characteristic of up-unweighting.

Try both styles in deep powder. Which seems better suited to bottomless snow? My own preference is for the extension-retraction turn, especially when snow is thick and heavy. Visualize the skis diving deep as you straighten your legs to the side, then floating across the hill as you retract your legs and let the lightened skis cross under your body toward the next turn.

Up-unweighted turn

Extension-retraction turn

13
RACING

The best skiers got that way through racing. Racing provides tremendous discipline. First, it makes you turn according to the rhythm of the race course, rather than to your own rhythm, and since every course is different the racer quickly develops a new level of versatility. Second, racing encourages the skier to learn and use a pure carved turn, a turn with no sideways braking component. Any sideskid costs time, so the successful racer turns without braking. Finally, racing provides immediate feedback. You learn after every run how well you're skiing: the clock tells you. A lower time means you're learning a smoother, more efficient technique. A higher time means you've blown it. And we all learn faster with frequent and immediate feedback.

Most skiers will start out racing on an easy giant slalom course. A typical first-time competition is the National Standard Race (NASTAR), which most ski areas set on a smooth low-intermediate run, with gates spaced easily along a section meant to provide a 20- to 30-second time for the experienced racer. The NASTAR course is neither technically challenging nor intimidating. Any wedge turn skier can negotiate the course. However, to ski it fast, you need to ski efficiently. First off, you need to ski a smooth line.

G R E E N

THE LINE

At first glance, race course gates appear to show you where to turn, but they're a bit misleading. Fast skiers start their turns well above each gate, and if the course is tight and twisty the expert racer arrives at each gate with most of the turn completed. It's more useful to think of the gates as traffic signs roughly outlining the course. You have to pass through each gate, but the gate shouldn't dictate where the turn starts. Instead, begin and end the turn wherever you'll get the smoothest, fastest line.

What a racer seeks to avoid is starting the turn too late. Too late a start puts you too low on the course, and in order to manage the gate you wind up slamming your skis sideways in a braking motion so you can scramble across the hill. This costs time. Getting low, or getting late, on even one or two gates will lose you the race.

The trick is to start turns high and early so you can ski a round, smooth turn on every gate. In a typical NASTAR course you should plan to have your skis in the fall line at each gate. In a tighter course, where you have to go farther across the hill, plan to be about two-thirds through the turn by the time you reach the gate.

Watch the other racers. The best skiers are deep into the turn at the gate, compressed and edging hard, ready to spring

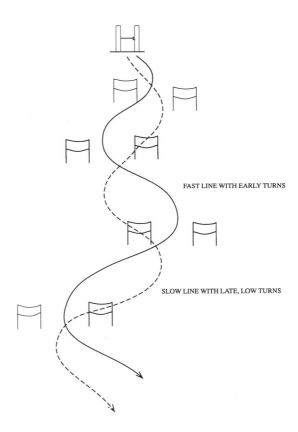

FAST LINE WITH EARLY TURNS

SLOW LINE WITH LATE, LOW TURNS

The line

for the next gate. The slowest skiers reach the gate (with some sense of relief) after a traverse from below the last gate.

One of the nice things about NASTAR is that the first skier down the course in the morning will be the pacesetter, usually one of the fastest racers on the mountain. The track set by the pacesetter in the freshly groomed snow is close to being the ideal fast line. If you can arrange to be the next skier out of the starting gate, following the pacesetter's track will show you all you need to know about the fast line down that course.

Later in the day, after several dozen skiers have been through the course, ruts develop around the gates. Chatter marks in the hard snow below each gate may make it tough to hold a good edgeset. In this case, it often pays to start the turn high and early, in order to finish the turn on smoother snow above the chatter marks. Finishing below the chatter marks will make you late for every gate.

B L U E

DIVERGING STEP

In Chapter Six we discussed the importance of balancing on one ski at a time on hard snow. The same is true for the race course. Fast skiers skate from ski to ski, powering each turn with the inside ski completely unweighted. From this derives the maximum arc and edgehold from the weighted ski. Look at the photo of the racer and see how the outside ski is fully flexed, while the inside ski is actually off the snow.

Transferring weight from one ski to the other as the new turn starts gives the racer a chance to accelerate. The weight transfer is similar to the strong skating motion made by a speed skater or hockey player accelerating across the ice.

Practice skating on a smooth, flat slope. Without using your poles, push off the edge of the left ski onto the right ski. As in skating, the tracks of the two skis must diverge slightly, because it's the outward thrust that develops forward momentum. Skate across the flat area smoothly, and gradually increase the pace. As the speed increases, you'll find you get better power through swinging the arms like a speed skater. To improve your strength, practice skating up a small incline, perhaps up the beginner hill.

*Diverging step
(racing step) turn*

Efficient skating is a matter of timing the push-off and balancing on the new ski. For maximum speed, the motion of the upper body should be forward rather than sideways, along the trajectory of the forward-moving new ski.

Now move this skating motion onto a gentle downhill slope. Slow down the pace: as you transfer your weight to the new ski, roll it into a gentle turn. Stabilize the end of the turn, and then skate off again onto a new ski.

Notice a few things: as you skate off the downhill ski onto the uphill ski, you cross over to start the new turn. This means the new ski starts off on its uphill edge and then rolls over into the new edgeset as you steer it toward the fall line. It also means that you've gained a little elevation with the skating step. That can be useful, since your skating acceleration carries you farther across the hill and you get to start the turn more directly above the next gate. This provides a longer, faster arc through the gate, and dramatically faster racecourse times.

As soon as you start skating from turn to turn you'll notice you're going a lot faster. Essentially, you've eliminated the braking function at the end of the turn and converted it into a muscle-powered acceleration.

Now take the skating step onto the racecourse. You'll have to slightly adapt the timing to match the rhythm of the gates. But done smoothly, with a clean arc, the skating turn can gain a couple of seconds on a 30-second course. Done powerfully, it can win the race.

B L A C K

JUMP START

In 1967, Jean–Claude Killy won the World Cup in all three disciplines: slalom, giant slalom and downhill. One of his tools was a sort of broad-jump start he invented. It shot him out of the starting gate so fast that he was nearly up to average speed before the first gate, on slalom and GS courses. And it gave him an advantage of roughly one second over racers who hadn't yet learned to vault out of the gate. Today, every serious racer learns the jump start; there's no way to win without it.

If you shuffle through the starting wand and depend on your own skating power and gravity for initial acceleration, the clock will start before you've even reached a normal walking speed of about two miles per hour. With the vault start, your upper body can be moving about ten miles per hour before your feet hit the starting wand; the feet are quick to catch up.

Here's how it's done. Move up to the starting wand and carefully plant your poles in the snow on the other side of the wand. Crouch comfortably, thighs horizontal but balanced on the balls of your feet. Visualize a broad jumper about to take off.

When the starter says "go," leap up and forward, and as your feet leave the snow kick them backward. This does two things: it moves your feet away from the wand so they don't trigger the clock to start too soon, and it propels your upper body forward over your ski poles. Now push down and back on your poles to accelerate downslope toward the first gate. Your feet trip the wand and you're moving. Fast.

Racing jump start

GLOSSARY

Abstem: An outward skidding motion: the tail of the outside ski skids at the end of a turn. Usually inadvertent, the abstem can be used purposely as a braking motion. In German, the term literally means "down stem," or stemming of the downhill ski.

Avalement: Originally, a racing turn in which the skier jets the skis forward, loading their tails and accelerating into the next turn. It has come to mean a turn in which the skier "swallows" or absorbs a bump by flexing the ankles, knees and hips, while changing edges and steering the skis "a val," or, "toward the valley."

Christie: A Christiania turn, or tail-skidded turn, with the skis parallel and edged only slightly.

Couloir: A narrow steep gulley or snow chute, usually between rocky outcrops.

Crossover: An edge change accomplished by projecting the upper body across the skis and toward the valley.

Deadfall: Logs, broken branches and fallen trees hidden beneath the snow, ready to snag the luckless powder skier.

Fall line: An imaginary line drawn straight down the hill. Think of the fall line as the route taken by a volleyball if you were to release it onto the snow surface.

Mogul: A hard bump in the snow, created by the passage of many skiers. Each time a skier carves a turn, it cuts away some snow from the troughs around the bump, deepening the troughs, thereby making the bump seem higher. The word mogul comes from a word in the Austrian dialect, "muggel," meaning a small hump.

Schuss: A straight run down the slope, with skis parallel to the fall line. The opposite of a traverse.

Stem: Outward displacement of the ski tail from the parallel position. You can stem the uphill ski (as at the beginning of a stem christie turn), the downhill ski (as in an abstem) or both skis at once (as in a wedge christie).

Traverse: To move across the hill, (as opposed to down the hill).

Tree well: When snow falls on a pine tree, the outward sloping branches serve as a tent, shedding the snow away from the tree trunk. A deep hole or well grows around the trunk, often all the way to the ground. A skier who falls through the branches and into the hole may be trapped there, especially if he goes in headfirst.

Unweighting: Any motion or maneuver that serves to lighten the pressure between the skis and the snow. Unweighting helps get the turn started because it permits easier steering and edge change. Common forms of unweighting include up-unweighting (rising tall), down-unweighting (a quick flexing of the ankles, knees and hips), and terrain unweighting (guiding the skis over a hump in the snow).

Wedge: A stable position for beginner skiers, with the tips of the skis together, the tails apart and the bases held flat on the snow surface. A wedge turn is an easy, slow turn steered from this position. We used to call the turn a snowplow, back in the days when we edged the skis hard and depended on the opposed edges for braking power.

Appendix:

MOUNTAIN SAFETY

Whenever you contemplate skiing something unfamiliar or intimidating, there's a strong impulse to stop at the top and inspect it. This is, in fact, a very good idea. Pausing gives you the chance to plan a smooth, safe line and visualize your technique. The best skiers in the world do it all the time, in order to memorize racecourses or figure out how to descend a couloir safely.

However, one of the most common (and distressing) sights at any ski area is a dense knot of stationary skiers standing smack in the middle of a trail where it breaks over into a steeper pitch. They've stopped to rest, to gossip, to inspect the difficult terrain on the far side. To a skier descending upon them from above, they look like a roadblock—an obstacle with the potential to move right or left unpredictably.

No driver would stop in the middle of a freeway. Instead, you pull to the side of the road and turn on the flashers. But skiers often feel free to stop anyplace on a crowded trail. The proper, safe and courteous thing to do is to turn to a stop at the edge of the trail, away from the flow of skier traffic.

One sad fact of life on the mountain is that the leading cause of fractures nowadays is skier collisions. We'd all be a lot safer if every skier followed the common sense Skier Responsibility Code:

▲ Ski in control. Ski so you can stop safely and avoid obstacles (including other skiers) below you. This rule is analogous to traffic laws that forbid speeding and reckless driving.

▲ When you stop, do it at the side of the trail, out of the traffic flow but in full view of skiers descending from above. If you stop below a breakover, there's always the chance that a skier speeding over the rise will hit you. It's a potentially fatal situation.

▲ When you enter a trail, or start skiing again after a trailside stop, look uphill for oncoming traffic. You wouldn't pull onto a highway without waiting for a break in traffic, but skiers unfortunately do it all the time.

▲ When you're skiing, it's your responsibility to keep from hitting skiers below you. In other words, if you rearend someone, it's your fault.

▲ Obey closure and warning signs.

▲ Use ski brakes or runaway straps, which are designed to protect other skiers from your flyaway equipment.

▲ Don't use drugs or alcohol while skiing. Most ski areas serve wine and beer at the cafeteria, but remember that if you live at sea level you can get pretty tipsy on one beer imbibed at high altitude. Save the drinking for après ski.

Skiing the uncrowded steep powder runs carries its own risks. Some simple rules for survival in high-angle terrain:

▲ Never ski alone in the woods or in avalanche country. A group of three or more is safest, because if one skier is hurt, another can go for help while the third looks after the injured party.

▲ Any broad, open slope of natural snow carries the potential of avalanche. Don't linger in the middle of this kind of terrain. When you must cross a steep powder chute or bowl, ski one at a time. Each member of the group should carry a snow shovel and an avalanche transceiver.

▲ On very steep terrain, be prepared to do a self-arrest. It's pretty simple. If you fall and begin to slide, roll onto your chest and use both hands to drive the point of one pole into the snow as a brake. Even if it doesn't stop you, this will swing your feet downhill so you'll slide into obstructions feet first instead of headfirst.

▲ On any trip into the back country, leave word with a reliable friend or the ski patrol regarding your planned route and expected time of arrival back home. Give yourself plenty of time to return before dark.

▲ If you get lost, or if someone is injured, keep everyone dry and get out of the wind. Dig a snowcave or use a tree well for shelter. The major danger is always hypothermia, that potentially fatal lowering of the body's core temperature. If you can stay dry and avoid windchill, however, chances for overnight survival are excellent.

▲ Parka pockets should contain some basic survival tools: a candy bar, a pocket knife, an extra hat.

First-aid instruction is beyond the scope of this book, but a few simple rules should be uppermost in your mind at all times.

▲ Don't move an injured skier until you're sure that there is no head, neck or spine damage. This is especially important with an unconscious skier. In any case, it's best to wait until the skier feels able to move under his own power; then you can assist.

▲ Stop severe bleeding promptly, using pressure on the wound.

▲ If you suspect a fracture, stabilize the injured limb but don't try to straighten or set it.

▲ Know how to perform CPR and how to treat for shock. If you don't know how, take a Red Cross first-aid course.

▲ Even a minor sprain can be life-threatening if the weather threatens hypothermia. Regardless of whether the injury is major or minor, it's vital to keep the victim dry and warm.

INDEX

About the Author

Seth Masia is a free-lance writer and a certified ski instructor. He began skiing on the glaciers above Chamonix, France, in the summer of 1968. In 1974 he joined the staff of *SKI Magazine*, and in 1983 began teaching at the Squaw Valley Ski School. Writing assignments have taken him around the world to ski.

Masia's ski-related books include *SKI Magazine's Total Skiing* (coauthored with Bob Jonas), *Alpine Ski Maintenance and Repair,* and *Cross Country Ski Maintenance and Repair.* He writes regularly for *SKI, Outside,* and a number of other magazines. In 1989 he won the Harold Hirsch Award, presented by the United States Ski Association for outstanding ski journalism.

He lives in Truckee, California, with his wife Stacey (herself a retired ski instructor), their daughter Cleo and numerous pets. When he can't ski, Masia writes on cycling, climbing and flying.